THE PIT AND THE PENDULUM
and Other Stories

A man is lying in a prison in Toledo. He is afraid – no, he is more than afraid, he is full of terror, because he knows that the Inquisition has many surprises in its prisons. Very soon he will look down into the pit . . .

And he is not the only person in these stories to be full of terror. When Fortunato meets his old friend Montresor, he is a happy man, on his way to a carnival party. But Montresor wants to talk about some Amontillado, and Fortunato finds himself in the cold damp vaults below Montresor's house. Terror soon follows . . .

The man who fears burial alive is never free from terror; a meeting of young lovers brings terror to many people; and the beautiful young wife of a painter sits smiling, smiling, smiling – but with terror in her heart.

Death and Terror, Terror and Death, walk hand in hand through these stories. Read them by daylight, in a bright sunny room, with friends around you!

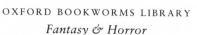

OXFORD BOOKWORMS LIBRARY
Fantasy & Horror

The Pit and the Pendulum
and Other Stories
Stage 2 (700 headwords)

Series Editor: Jennifer Bassett
Founder Editor: Tricia Hedge
Activities Editors: Jennifer Bassett and Christine Lindop

EDGAR ALLAN POE

The Pit and the Pendulum

and Other Stories

Retold by
John Escott

Illustrated by
Ian Miller

OXFORD UNIVERSITY PRESS

OXFORD
UNIVERSITY PRESS

Great Clarendon Street, Oxford OX2 6DP

Oxford University Press is a department of the University of Oxford.
It furthers the University's objective of excellence in research, scholarship,
and education by publishing worldwide in

Oxford New York

Auckland Cape Town Dar es Salaam Hong Kong Karachi
Kuala Lumpur Madrid Melbourne Mexico City Nairobi
New Delhi Shanghai Taipei Toronto

With offices in

Argentina Austria Brazil Chile Czech Republic France Greece
Guatemala Hungary Italy Japan Poland Portugal Singapore
South Korea Switzerland Thailand Turkey Ukraine Vietnam

OXFORD and OXFORD ENGLISH are registered trade marks of
Oxford University Press in the UK and in certain other countries

ISBN-13: 978 0 19 423308 8
ISBN-10: 0 19 423308 1

Printed in China.

CONTENTS

The Pit
and the Pendulum

I will not open my eyes. Not yet. I lie on my back, very still, and remember . . .

The black clothes of the judges . . . their voices, their words. *You must die* . . . I watched the judges' mouths – mouths speaking my name, ordering my death. *You must die* . . . Cold hands of terror closed round my heart. Then came a sweet thought – what wonderful rest there will be in the grave! After that, I fainted, and saw and heard nothing for a long while.

But I knew when they took me away from that room. They were tall men, moving silently. Down . . . down they carried me, down into darkness and terror.

I have not opened my eyes yet. I lie on my back, and put out my hand. It falls heavily on something wet and hard. Where am I? Am I still in the prisons at Toledo? Why am I still alive? The Spanish Inquisition kills by fire. Why have they not burnt me to death?

And now I remember other stories of the prisons at Toledo, stories of other kinds of death . . .

I am afraid to open my eyes. Not afraid of seeing

something terrible, but afraid that there is nothing to see. And when at last I do open them, I am right. The blackness of the blackest night is around me. Am I already dead? No! A terrible thought comes to me. I am in a tomb – they have buried me alive in a tomb!

A terrible thought comes to me. I am in a tomb . . .

I jump up, moving my arms around me. I can feel and see nothing. This place is too big to be a tomb.

I walk on, slowly, until my fingers touch a wall. It is wet and cold. I begin to follow it round, but then stop. How big is my prison? I must know. I tear off a small piece of my long prison shirt and put it on the floor, next to the wall. I move on again, counting my steps.

Walking is not easy. My feet often slip on the wet floor, and suddenly I fall down. I lie there, with my eyes closed. I want to get up, but I am tired . . . so tired . . .

I sleep for some time. When I wake up, I put out my arm and find bread and a bottle of water next to me. I eat hungrily and drink from the bottle. After a time, I get up and follow the wall again, counting my steps.

When I find the piece of my shirt on the floor, I stop and think. My prison is about fifty steps around – so about thirty metres. Does it help me to know this? Perhaps not, but now I want to know more.

I start to move across the room, away from the wall. After six or seven steps, my feet slip on the wet floor again, and I fall heavily on my face.

And yet . . . there is nothing under my head. My body lies on the floor, but under my head there is . . . nothing. And I can feel on my face a little soft wind, bringing with it a smell, a warm wet smell – the smell of things that have been dead for a long time.

3

I put out my arm, and find that I am on the edge of a pit. How deep is it? I feel around the floor with my fingers and find a small stone. I drop it into the pit, and listen. After a long time, it falls into water.

At the same moment, a door opens and closes high above me. For a second there is light in my prison, and then it is gone again. But in that second I see I was just one step away from death in that terrible pit.

Shaking, I move slowly back to the wall. I have heard stories about the prison pits of the Inquisition, and they do not give you a quick, clean death.

Dear God, I am going to die in this prison – a slow and terrible death. Every second of every hour of every day I will wait for it, and the waiting will be as terrible as the death itself.

My fear keeps me from sleep for many long hours, but at last my eyes close. When I wake up, there is bread and water beside me again. So . . . they are watching me all the time, and come in while I am asleep.

I am very thirsty and I drink the water quickly. They have put something in it because at once I feel very sleepy, and I fall into a long, deep sleep. For how long, I do not know. But when I wake up, it is not so dark. A yellow light is coming from somewhere, and I can see my prison at last.

The room is square, and the walls are not made of

stone but of metal. There are pictures on them, pictures
of faces with wild-looking eyes – the eyes of devils. In the
centre of the stone floor is the pit.

I cannot stand up! Why?

Now I see. I am lying on my back, and am tied to a low
wooden bed, with many ropes around my body. I can
move my head a little, and my right arm, and I can just
get a hand to the plate of food on the floor next to me.
But there is no bottle of water . . . and I am so thirsty. The
food this time is meat, dry salty meat, which makes me
even thirstier than I was before.

I look up at the metal ceiling above me. On one square
of it there is a picture of old Father Time. He is holding a
pendulum . . . No, wait! The pendulum is *real* – it is
moving from side to side.

I watch it for a while, a little afraid. Then I hear a
noise. Nine or ten large rats have come up from the pit.
They can smell the meat, and are running to it across the
floor. I make them go away again, but it is hard work.

Because of the rats it is about an hour before I look up
at the ceiling again. The pendulum is still moving from
side to side, but more strongly now, and . . . yes! It is
getting lower! Then I go cold with terror. I see that the
bottom of the pendulum is made of a great piece of
metal, bright and sharp – sharper than the blade of any
knife. It is right above my heart, and when it moves from

side to side through the air, the blade makes a terrible *hissing* noise.

And with each move, it comes nearer and nearer.

I escaped death in the pit, but now I am staring at another death. I can do nothing, only watch in terror, and wait until that bright blade cuts into my body.

With each move of the pendulum, that bright blade comes nearer and nearer.

Hours, perhaps days, go past. I do not know how many, but the terror does not stop.

I have counted the moves of the pendulum . . . watched the blade come lower and lower . . . heard the hissing get louder and louder. Already I can smell the metal of the sharp blade, and I push my body up to it.

'Come! Cut me! Be quick, give me death!'

I sleep, wake, and sleep again. And still the pendulum moves from side to side above me, and the blade comes nearer and nearer. When it reaches me, it will cut across my body, into my heart.

I cannot stop watching it now. I cry out, I laugh, I scream, and still the blade comes nearer. So many long hours of terror. When will they end?

I am hungry, and put out my hand to take the last piece of meat from the plate on the floor. *Wait!*

A thought comes into my head.

Could I . . .?

It is only a small hope, but . . .

The rats are still with me, waiting around my bed, watching me with their red, hungry eyes. 'What food', I think, 'do they eat in that terrible pit?'

They can smell the piece of meat in my hand. I can see their eyes, watching. The meat is full of fat, and if I put the fat on the ropes around my body . . .

I do this. Then I lie still.

Yes! Some of the biggest rats have jumped up on me. Now there are more, coming from the pit. Suddenly there are hundreds of them running over me, over my body, over my face, touching my eyes, my mouth with their cold mouths. Aaagh!

In seconds the blade will begin to cut into me. I must lie still, I must lie still . . .

And yes! The rats are eating into the ropes – I can feel it! The blade of the pendulum begins to cut my shirt, and now my body, but the rats have done their work and the ropes fall away from me.

I push the rats off, move away from the pendulum, off the bed, onto the floor. There! I am free!

Free – but still a prisoner of the Inquisition.

The pendulum has stopped moving. It is going back up through the ceiling. So, they are still watching me. What new terror will they send me now?

I look around my metal prison. Already, something is different, something has changed. What is it? And this yellow light, where is it coming from? I look again at the metal walls – and now I can see the narrow gap along the bottom. The yellow light comes from there. I get down to look, but cannot see through the gap.

When I stand up again, I see at once what is different. Those faces on the walls . . . the colours are brighter, and those wild, devilish eyes burn with – with fire. Yes, real fire! The walls and ceiling are burning, and the smell of hot metal fills the prison. Already it is hard to breathe.

I move away from the wall to the pit in the centre of the room. The burning ceiling sends light deep into the pit, and looking down, I see . . .

Looking down into the pit, I see . . .

No, no, I cannot – I cannot speak of it! Not this! No, no, not this! Oh, any terror, but not this!

I run from the edge and hide my face in my hands.

It is getting hotter, much hotter. Shaking, I take my hands away from my face and look up. What's this? The walls are *moving*. The room is changing, it is longer and narrower, the walls are closing in on me. So this is the new death – death by burning. Then come, Death! Any death is better than the pit!

But the burning walls push me nearer and nearer to the centre of the room – and the pit. Of course! That is what they want! The walls will push me until I fall *into the pit!* There will be no escape from this death.

So hot now, and getting hotter . . . the burning walls closing in . . . nowhere to stand . . . my back and arms are burnt . . . my feet are on the edge of the pit . . . I cannot hold . . . I give one last, long scream—

Voices! I can hear voices! Yes, and the sound of running feet, doors opening, men shouting. Now the burning walls are moving back. A hand catches my arm as I begin to fall, fainting, into the pit.

It is General Lasalle. The French army has arrived in the city of Toledo, and the Spanish Inquisition is at last in the hands of its enemies.

The Cask of Amontillado

Fortunato did and said a thousand things to hurt me. But when he insulted me, I knew that it was time to punish him. 'But I must do it cleverly and secretly,' I thought. 'Only Fortunato himself must know that I am punishing him.'

I was as friendly to Fortunato as before, of course. I went on smiling at him, and he did not know that I was smiling at the thought of his death.

Both he and I liked and bought fine wine. Fortunato knew very little about other things, but he did know about wine and sherry wine. And so did I.

One evening, during the city's carnival, I met my friend in the street. He was dressed in carnival clothes and smelled strongly of wine.

'My dear Fortunato!' I said. 'What luck to meet you! I have bought a cask of Amontillado – but now, well, I'm not so sure that it *is* Amontillado.'

'Amontillado?' said Fortunato. 'No, no! Nobody sells the best sherry in the middle of carnival. No, no, no!'

'I was stupid,' I said. 'I paid the full Amontillado price,

and did not ask you to try it first. But I couldn't find you, and I was afraid of losing it to another buyer. So, the cask is already in my vaults.'

'Amontillado!' he said.

'Perhaps,' I said. 'But I must be sure. I can see that

'I can see you are on your way to a carnival party.'

12

you are on your way to a carnival party. I'll go and see Luchresi. He will tell me—'

'Luchresi does not know the difference between Amontillado and any other sherry wine,' he said.

'Really? But some people say that he knows wine as well as you do.'

'Come, let's go,' he said.

'Where to?'

'To your vaults,' he said.

'My friend, no,' I said. 'I can hear that you have a bad cough, and my vaults are terribly cold and wet.'

'My cough is nothing,' Fortunato said. 'Let's go. Amontillado! Never! Your wine-seller is stealing your money. And as for Luchresi – what does he know about Amontillado?'

He took my arm, and we walked quickly to my house.

There was no one at home because my servants were out enjoying themselves at the carnival. I took Fortunato through the building and down the stairs into the vaults. Here were the tombs of the Montresors – my family.

'The Amontillado?' Fortunato said. He began to cough in the cold, damp air.

'It's further on,' I said. 'How long have you had that cough?'

He went on coughing for some time before he could answer me. 'It is nothing,' he said, at last.

My friend was full of wine, and found walking difficult. The little bells on his carnival suit made ringing noises when he moved. He began to cough again.

'We'll go back,' I said. 'You must not get ill. You have family, friends, you are loved, needed – you must take care of yourself. We'll go back. I can go to Luchresi—'

'Stop!' he said. 'The cough is nothing. It will not kill me. I shall not die from a cough.'

'That's true,' I said. 'But you must be careful. Take a drink from this bottle of Medoc. It is a good wine and will warm you. Here you are, drink this!'

I opened the bottle and gave it to him. 'I drink,' he said, 'to all the dead Montresors sleeping around us.' And he drank.

'And I drink to your long life,' I said.

Again he took my arm and we walked on.

'These vaults are very large,' he said.

'The Montresor family is a very old one. There have been a great many of us.'

I was warmed by the Medoc, and the wine was making Fortunato's eyes bright. We walked on, past casks and bottles of wine, deep into the vaults. I stopped again and held his arm.

'We are under the river now,' I said. 'See how wet the walls are here. Come, we will go back before it is too late. Your cough—'

'It is nothing,' he said. 'Let's go on. But first, another drink to keep us warm.'

I took another bottle of wine and gave it to him. He drank it all without stopping. His eyes were even brighter, and he laughed.

'Now, let's go on to the Amontillado,' he said.

We walked on, deep into the vaults.

We went on, and down, and came into the deepest vault. Around three walls, from floor to ceiling, were the bones of the dead. Many more bones lay on the floor. Cut into the fourth wall was a smaller vault.

Fortunato held up his torch and looked into the blackness, but could see nothing.

'Go in,' I told him. 'You will find the Amontillado in there.'

He went inside and I followed him. In three steps he was at the back wall of the vault, and he stood there, looking stupid. On the wall were two metal rings and a chain with a lock. Before he could do anything, I put the chain around him and locked it to the rings.

'Put your hand on the wall, Fortunato,' I said. 'How wet it is! How *very* wet! Once more I ask, why don't you go back? No? Then I must leave you. But first I must try to make you comfortable.'

'The – the Amontillado!' my friend said. He did not understand.

'True,' I said. 'The Amontillado.'

Hidden under some of the bones on the floor were stones and other things for building a wall. I took them across to the small vault and began to work quickly.

Before the wall was half a metre high, Fortunato began to make soft crying noises. Then he was silent for some time. I worked on busily, building the wall higher and higher. Then I heard him again. He was pulling the chain and shaking it, but I knew the lock was strong.

The wall was now as high as my neck. I held my torch higher, to see his face. He began to scream, long high screams, filled with terror. I listened, worrying. No, we were too deep under the ground. No sounds would escape from this vault. I screamed back at Fortunato, longer and louder. Then he stopped.

I held my torch higher, to see his face.

17

By midnight the wall was nearly finished. There was one last heavy stone. I had it almost in place when I heard a soft but terrible laugh.

Then Fortunato's sad voice said, 'Ha! Ha! Ha! A very good joke. We will laugh about it often when we are drinking our wine.'

'The Amontillado!' I said.

'Ha! Ha! Yes, the Amontillado. But it is getting late. My wife and friends are waiting for me. Let's go now, Montresor.'

'Yes,' I said. 'Let's go.'

'For the love of God, Montresor!'

'Yes,' I said. 'For the love of God.'

I waited for an answer. None came.

'Fortunato!' I called.

No answer. I called again.

'Fortunato!'

Still no answer. I pushed my torch through the gap in the wall and let it fall. Still nothing. I put the last stone in place, and then in front of the new wall I put the bones of the dead.

For fifty years, nobody has moved them.

The Premature Burial

What is the most horrible thing that can happen to a person? It is not death, but premature burial – burial *before* death, burial while you are still *alive*. It is everyone's worst fear.

Life and Death. When does one end, and the other begin? With some illnesses, we cannot be sure. The body is cold and still, the heart has stopped, breathing has stopped . . . but this is not always the end of a life.

So it is not difficult to understand why premature burials sometimes happen. People still remember the story of a Baltimore woman, not long ago. She went to her bed with a sudden illness, and died soon after.

Or so her husband and her doctors thought.

Her heart was silent, her face grey, her eyes unseeing, her body as cold as the grave. She lay like this for three days, and then they buried her in the family vault.

Three years later, they opened the vault again for another coffin. When her husband pulled back the doors, something fell noisily into his arms.

It was his wife's skeleton, in her white burial clothes.

19

Doctors thought that the woman 'came alive' again about two days after her burial. She fought wildly to get out of her coffin, they said, until it fell and broke open. She then used a piece of the broken coffin to hit the metal doors of the vault. But nobody heard her, or her screams for help. Then perhaps she fainted, or even died of terror. Her burial dress caught on some metalwork, which stopped her falling. And so she stayed, standing dead at the door, for three years.

And so she stayed, standing dead at the door,
for three years.

How often are people buried alive? Perhaps more often than we know. Think of the terror of it – the smell of the cold damp ground . . . the blackness of the night inside the narrow coffin . . . the long, long silence.

There are many true stories about premature burials. This is the one that happened to me.

For some years I had an illness called catalepsy. People who have catalepsy lie still and do not move for hours, or even days. They are still warm, and there is still some colour in their faces, but you have to listen hard to hear their heart or their breathing. Sometimes they can stay like this for weeks or months. And then it is difficult to find life in them.

When a cataleptic fit started, I always felt cold and ill, and then I fainted. After this, everything was black and silent. I always woke up very slowly – and I could never remember anything about the fit.

My body itself was well and strong, but I began to worry more and more. I talked all the time about coffins and graves. Day and night my thoughts were about premature burial. I was afraid of sleeping – and afraid of waking up in a grave. And when at last I did fall asleep, my dreams were about the terrors of death.

Once I dreamed that I was in a long cataleptic fit. A cold hand touched my face, and a voice in my ear said softly, 'Get up!'

I sat up. Everything was dark and I could not see the speaker. Where was I? The cold hand started to shake my arm, and the voice said, 'Get up! I said, get up!'

'Who are you?' I asked.

'I have no name in the place where I live,' said the voice. 'I was alive, but now I am dead, and a thing of darkness. I cannot sleep, cannot rest. How can *you* sleep so quietly? Get up! Come with me into the night, and I will show you the graves of the dead.'

And in my dream I looked into the open graves of every dead person in the world. I saw them, sleeping the long sleep of death in their burial clothes. But more terrible than the dead were the not-dead – those who were not sleeping, those who were fighting to get out of their coffins, those who died trying to escape.

While I stared, the voice spoke to me again. 'It is a most terrible thing to see, a most terrible thing . . .'

I remembered these dreams for a long time. I began to be afraid to leave my house. I did not want to be away from people who knew about my cataleptic fits. My friends, I thought, will never bury me alive by mistake. But then I began to worry about my friends . . .

So I made many changes in my family vault. Usually the doors opened from outside; now I could open them from inside. I made holes for air and light to come in, and places for food and water near the coffin. I bought a new coffin that was warm and comfortable. The top of the coffin was like a door, and I could open it from the inside. And on the ceiling of the vault I put a big bell, with a rope that came down to the coffin, and through a hole in the top, next to my hand.

But I was still afraid . . .

I made many changes in my family vault.

And I was right to be afraid. One day I woke up slowly, eyes still closed, feeling strangely tired. Then a sudden terror hit me. I tried to think, to remember . . . and then I felt that I was waking up not from sleep, but from a cataleptic fit. And cold fear filled me at once, fear that never leaves me, day or night.

For some minutes I lay still, but at last I opened my eyes. It was dark – all dark – the darkness of a night that would never end. I felt that I lay on hard wood, and when I moved my arms, they hit wood on both sides of me, and above my face.

I was lying in a coffin.

Then hope came. I pushed hard to open the top of my special coffin; it would not move. I tried to find the bell-rope; it was not there. And now hope left me. This was a hard wooden coffin, not my soft, comfortable one. And there was a smell of wetness, a smell of cold damp ground! I was *not* in my vault . . .

'Oh, dear God!' I thought. 'I have had a cataleptic fit, and I'm away from my home and with people who don't know me. They think that I'm dead, and they have buried me like a dog, in a cheap wooden coffin. Deep, deep in a grave with no name on it! No, no!'

I screamed – a long, wild, terrible scream.

'Hello? Hello?' a man's voice answered.

'What's the matter?' said a second man's voice.

'What's going on?' said a third man's voice. 'Why are you screaming like that?'

Then the men began to shake me. They did not wake me, because I was already awake, but the shaking helped me, and at once I remembered everything.

I was near Richmond, in Virginia, on a walk with a friend beside the James River. When night came, there was a sudden storm. We saw an old sailing boat at the side of the river, and hurried along to it.

'We must get out of this storm,' I said to my friend. 'The boat is very small, but it will keep us dry.'

So we slept there that night. The beds were very narrow, and were not much better than long wooden boxes in the side of the boat. They were only half a metre across, and half a metre from top to bottom. It was difficult to get into a bed that was so small, but I slept well . . . and dreamt.

In my dream – and of course it *was* a dream – my narrow wooden bed became my coffin. The damp smell came from the river and the wet ground after the rain. And the men who shook me to wake me up were the workmen on the boat.

It was a dream, yes. But the *terror* was real, and terror can make people ill, or even kill them. But something good came from this terrible adventure. After that day I stopped thinking about death and burial. I went walking

In my dream my narrow wooden bed became my coffin.

and riding, and breathed the free air. My fears went away, and my catalepsy went with them.

It is easy to understand the terror of a living burial, the terror of waking inside a closed coffin. But we must put away thoughts like these, and close the door on them, or fear and worry will send us to an early grave.

The Meeting

How well I remember that meeting! I was in Venice, that city of dark secrets and silent waters. It was midnight, and the midsummer air was hot and still, the canals silent and empty.

I was coming home in a gondola along the Grand Canal when I heard a sudden scream – a woman's scream. I jumped up, and the boatman turned my gondola to go under the Bridge of Sighs and past the great house of the Mentoni family. Lights were on in all the windows, and people were running down the steps to the water. The canal was suddenly as light as day.

'What has happened?' I called out.

'A child fell from its mother's arms,' came the answer. 'From a high window of the house.'

I stopped to watch, full of fear for the child. Already people were swimming in the water, calling, shouting, looking everywhere.

At the doorway to the palace stood the child's young mother, the Marchesa di Mentoni, the loveliest woman in all of Venice.

She stood alone. But she was not looking into the water for her lost child. She was staring across the canal at the building opposite. Why? I asked myself. What could she see there, in the dark corners of that old building? Or was she afraid to look into the canal, afraid to see the dead body of her child in the dark waters?

On the steps behind the Marchesa, higher up, stood her old husband, Mentoni himself, the head of the rich and famous Mentoni family. He gave orders to the servants who were looking for his child, but he looked bored, bored to death.

Then, from one of the dark corners outside the building opposite, a man stepped into the light and immediately jumped into the canal.

A minute later, he stood next to the Marchesa with the living, breathing child in his arms. The light from the windows fell on his face, and everyone could see him.

He was a very famous young man – as beautiful as a Greek god, with his black eyes, and his wild black hair. We were not close friends, but I knew him a little, from my time in Venice.

He did not speak. And to my great surprise the Marchesa did not take her child in her arms and hold him close. Other hands took the child and carried him away, into the house. And the Marchesa? Her eyes were wet with tears, and her hands were shaking.

*The young man stood next to the Marchesa
with the child in his arms.*

Then old Mentoni turned and went into the house. The Marchesa took the young man's hand in both of hers, and stared into his face. Her eyes were dark with terror, and her face as white as the moonlight that danced on the waters of the canal.

She spoke softly, hurriedly, the tears running down that wild, white face. Below the steps, in my gondola, I heard every word.

'You have won,' she said, 'you have won . . . and you are right . . . there is only one answer . . . we cannot go on . . . we agreed the way, and now the time has come . . . we shall meet . . . one hour after sunrise . . .'

✠ ✠ ✠

Everyone went away, lights went out, and my young friend now stood alone on the steps. He was white-faced and shaking. He looked around and saw me, and remembered me at once.

There were no other boats on the canal at that time, so I took him home in my gondola. We talked of unimportant things, and then he asked me to visit him the next morning.

'Come at sunrise,' he said. 'Yes, at sunrise! Not a minute later. Please!'

I thought his words were a little strange, but they were not the first strange words on that strange night.

I agreed to go, and arrived at sunrise. His apartment

was in one of those very old buildings which look down on the Grand Canal, near the Rialto Bridge. The rooms were large, and full of beautiful things from Italy, Greece, Egypt . . . There were pictures, furniture, carpets, things made of black stone, and red stone, of glass, of gold, of silver . . . Soft music was playing somewhere, and the early morning sunlight danced in through the windows.

There was too much to look at, too much light, too many colours, too many beautiful things. I stared around in silent surprise, and my young friend laughed.

'Oh, I am sorry for laughing,' he said. 'But you look so surprised! And sometimes a man *must* laugh or die. How wonderful to die laughing, don't you agree?'

He half-fell into a low chair, still laughing in that strange way.

'I have other apartments,' he went on, 'but none like this one. You are one of the very few people who have seen it. Come – I have some famous pictures here. You must see them.'

He wanted to show me everything. He was tired, but also excited. And perhaps afraid too. I could not be sure. But something was worrying him. Sometimes he stopped speaking in the middle of a sentence and listened. To what? The sound of another visitor on the stairs? To words inside his head?

During one of these silent moments, I turned away and saw a book of Italian songs on a small table. The open page was wet with new tears. And on the opposite, empty page, written in English and in my young friend's handwriting, were these lines:

> You were my sun, my moon, my stars,
>   My life I gave to you.
> We danced by day, we sang by night,
>   A love so sweet and true.
> Now all my days I spend in darkness,
>   The fire of life is cold,
> I see no more your quick bright smile,
>   Your hand I cannot hold.
> They took you from our English clouds
>   To a blue Italian sky,
> To marry an old man, rich in gold,
>   And now my heart will die.

Under these lines were written a place and date. The place was London. This surprised me, because when I first met him in Venice, I asked him, 'When you were living in London, did you ever meet the Marchesa di Mentoni? She lived in that city for some years before she married.'

To this he replied, 'I have never been to London.'

For a rich young Englishman I thought this was strange, but I thought little of it at the time.

He did not see me with this book, and now turned to me again.

'One more picture to see,' he said. 'Come.'

He took me to a small room. There was just one picture in it – a portrait of the Marchesa di Mentoni.

My young friend stood, staring at the portrait for a long time.

She stood, smiling down at us, as beautiful as ever, her dark eyes full of life.

My young friend stood, staring at the portrait for a long time. Then, at last, he said, 'Come, let's drink!'

He went away to find wine, and I turned back to the book of Italian songs on the little table. Perhaps there were answers to these mysteries about my friend in this book. I turned the pages, and found, hidden at the back of the book, part of a letter. It was in a woman's handwriting.

. . . You say that you love me, more than the world, more than life itself. But how much is that? How can I be sure? Will you do this for me? Will you save from death my child – my child, by *him*?

If you do this, then I will know that your words are true. And I will take your hand for one last time . . . We shall go together through that last door . . .

I heard a sound, and closed the book hurriedly. My friend came back into the room, carrying two large silver goblets, full to the top with wine. He gave one to me.

'It is early, but let's drink,' he said again. At that moment a clock sounded the hour. 'One hour after sunrise,' he said softly. 'Yes, it *is* early. But what does it matter? Let us drink to the sun, yes, the sun!'

He drank his goblet of wine very quickly.

'To dreams,' he said. 'All my life I have dreamed. I have made myself a home of dreams, here in the heart of Venice. Where could be better?' He put his empty goblet down on the table. 'And now I am ready for the land of *real* dreams. Soon, I shall be there . . .'

'All my life I have dreamed . . .'

He stopped and listened – but to what, I did not know. Then he lifted his head and said:

> Wait for me there! I will be sure
> To meet you at that last dark door.

On the last word he fell into a chair, and his eyes closed.

At the same moment there were feet on the stairs, and a loud knocking at the door. A young servant from the Mentoni house ran into the room.

'The Marchesa! I come from the Marchesa!' the boy cried. 'Poison! She has taken poison! She is *dead*!'

I ran to the chair and tried to wake my young friend, to tell him this strange and terrible news.

But he did not move. His hand was cold to my touch, and his face white and still.

He, too, was *dead*.

I fell back against the table in terror, and my hand touched my friend's wine goblet, which stood there. It was now blackened inside, and from it came a sweet, sickly smell – the smell of poison.

And in a second I understood everything.

The Oval Portrait

I was in the Italian mountains when I fell from my horse and hurt myself. I needed to rest but in that wild, lonely place there was only one house. It was a fine old building, very big, but dark and empty. My servant, Pedro, broke the lock on a door and helped me inside.

I looked around at the furniture, the carpets, the paintings. 'The people who lived here,' I thought, 'left only a short time ago.'

We used one of the smaller rooms in a far corner of the building. There were a great many modern paintings on the walls, and more in the dark corners of the room. It was getting dark and Pedro lit the tall candles on the table by my bed. There was a book on the table, and I began reading it. It described and told the story of each of the pictures on the walls.

Midnight came and went, and I moved the candles closer to me, to give a better light for reading. But the light also fell on one of the darker corners of the room – and there I saw for the first time an oval portrait of a beautiful young woman, just her head and shoulders. It was a very fine painting, but there was also something different about it, something strange, something . . . I did not know what it was, but I could not take my eyes away from that portrait. For about an hour I sat in the bed, staring at it.

It was a very fine painting,
but there was also something strange about it.

And at last I found its secret. It was in her face, in her eyes. 'She could easily be . . . *alive*,' I thought. 'She *looks* alive. Those eyes . . .'

Suddenly I felt cold, and a great fear filled me. My hands began to shake, and I had to look away.

Carefully, I moved the candles again until the light no longer fell in that corner, and the portrait went back into darkness. I found the place in the book which told the story of the oval portrait, and began to read.

✠   ✠   ✠

She was a young woman of great beauty, and even more beautiful when she was smiling and laughing.

It was a dark day when she saw, and loved, and married the painter. He was already famous for his art, and was always studying and working. The great love of his life was his work, his painting.

His beautiful young wife was playful, full of life and light and smiles, as happy and as loving as a child. But she learned to fear and then to hate everything about painting. Her husband's work was her enemy, because it kept him away from her, hour after hour.

So it was a terrible thing for her when he said he wanted to paint her portrait. But she agreed because she loved him and wanted to please him.

For many weeks she sat in a dark high room where the light from above fell onto the painting and onto her. Day after day,

*He painted hour after hour, not speaking a word,
thinking only of his work.*

she sat still and silent, not moving, not speaking. But she went on smiling and smiling because she saw that the painter loved his work so much.

He painted hour after hour, not speaking a word, thinking only of his work. Those who saw the portrait looked and said softly, 'It is your finest work. Oh, you do love her dearly! We can see this in the portrait.'

And it was true. But he did not look at her now. He went on working, more and more wildly, thinking and dreaming only of the portrait and never of his wife. Day by day she looked more and more unhappy, but he did not see it. Her face and body were now thin, but he did not see it. He took the warm colour from her face, and painted it into the face in his portrait – but he could not, he would not see it.

After many weeks, he finished. One last touch of paint on the mouth, a last touch to the eye . . .

The painter stood back and looked at the portrait of his wife. How wonderful it was! But while he stared, he began to shake and his face went white. Then he cried out with a loud voice, 'This is LIFE itself! She LIVES in this portrait!' and he turned suddenly to look at the woman he loved. She was dead!

GLOSSARY

apartment   a group of rooms in a building where you can live
bell   a metal thing that makes a noise when someone hits it
blade   the part of a knife that cuts
bone   one of the hard white parts inside your body
breathe   to take in or send out air through your nose and mouth
bury   to put a dead person in the ground; **burial** *(n)*
canal   a river made by people for boats to travel on
carnival   a party for everybody in the streets, with music,
     singing, and dancing
cask   a large wooden container for drink
catalepsy   an illness where people stay asleep and do not move
ceiling   the part of a room that is over your head
chain   a lot of metal rings joined together in a line
cough *(v & n)*   to send out air from the mouth in a noisy way
damp   a little bit wet
devil   a very bad spirit
dream *(n)*   pictures or ideas in your head when you are asleep
edge   the part along the end or side of something
faint *(v)*   to fall down suddenly because you are ill or afraid
fear *(n)*   what you feel when you are afraid
fit *(n)*   an illness when you faint and cannot control your body
furniture   tables, beds, chairs, etc.
gap   a space between two things
goblet   a cup without handles for drinking wine
grave   a place where a dead person is buried
heart   the part of your body that pushes the blood around
hiss *(v)*   to make a long 'ssss' sound
horrible   very bad, terrible; making you very afraid or unhappy

42

Inquisition   a group of Roman Catholic churchmen in the 16th century who punished people who did not agree with them

insult *(v)*   to say something bad about somebody

joke *(n)*   something you do or say to make people laugh

judge   a person in law who decides the punishments for bad people

low   not high

metal   something hard; gold, silver, steel, etc. are metals

order *(v)*   to tell someone to do something

oval *(adj)*   like the shape of an egg

pendulum   part of a machine that swings from side to side

pit   a large deep hole in the ground

poison   something that can kill you if you eat or drink it

premature   happening earlier than expected

punish   to hurt someone because they did something wrong

rope   very thick, strong string

save   to take someone or something out of danger

servant   someone who works in another person's house

sharp   with an edge that cuts easily (e.g. a sharp knife)

skeleton   the bones inside a person's body

slip *(v)*   to almost fall

stare   to look at someone or something for a long time

step *(v)*   one movement of your feet when you walk

sunrise   the time of day when the sun first appears

tears   water that comes from the eyes when you cry

terror   very great fear

thought *(n)*   something that you think

tie *(v)*   to put ropes round something to hold it still

tomb   a small stone building for a dead person

wine   an alcoholic drink made from grapes

Before Reading

1 **Read the story introduction on the first page of the book, and the back cover. How much do you know now about the stories? Tick one box for each sentence.**

		YES	NO
1	These stories will make you smile.	☐	☐
2	The man in Toledo is in prison.	☐	☐
3	Montresor wants to go to a carnival party.	☐	☐
4	Fortunato finds terror under the ground.	☐	☐
5	One man is afraid that they will bury him before he is dead.	☐	☐
6	When the two lovers meet, it is a happy day.	☐	☐
7	The painter's wife is a happy person.	☐	☐

2 **Here are the titles of the five stories. Which of the things in the list below belong to each story (two for each story)? Can you guess?**

a book about paintings / a broken coffin / a chain / an empty house / a letter / an old sailing boat / a sharp blade /some bottles of wine / some rats / Venice

The Pit and the Pendulum _____ _____

The Cask of Amontillado _____ _____

The Premature Burial _____ _____

The Meeting _____   _____
The Oval Portrait _____   _____

3 Can you guess what will happen in the stories? Choose endings for each of these sentences.

1 The man in the prison . . .
   a) will fall into the pit.
   b) will die of terror.
   c) will leave the prison alive.

2 After Fortunato and Montresor go to the vaults . . .
   a) only Fortunato will leave alive.
   b) only Montresor will leave alive.
   c) nobody will leave alive.

3 The man who is afraid of burial alive . . .
   a) will lose his fear.
   b) will die of terror.
   c) will go mad.

4 The two young lovers . . .
   a) will both die.
   b) will run away together.
   c) will kill someone.

5 When the painter finishes his work . . .
   a) he will die.
   b) his wife will die.
   c) he and his wife will die.

After Reading

1 **Perhaps this is what some of the characters in the stories are thinking. Complete each passage with the words from the list. Which characters are they, and what has just happened in the story?**

black / cannot / child / enough / have / lose / must / or / will

1 'There! I _____ done it! My _____ – my dearest son – is in the water, and I _____ turn back now. But _____ he come? Does he truly love me _____? The night is so _____, and the water is so cold. He _____ come soon – _____ I will _____ my child, my love, my hope . . .'

This is _____, and _____

behind / death / door / feel / him / moving / once / pit / rats / somebody

2 'Are there any more prisoners here? What's _____ these walls? They _____ hot – and, yes, they're _____! Is that the _____? Quickly – we must open it at _____! Ugh! There are _____ everywhere, big and fat. And that smell – it's the smell of _____. But look – there's _____ in the middle, near the _____. Can I get to _____ in time?'

This is _____, and _____

anywhere / chain / doing / hand / here / perhaps / wet / understand

3 'Why has he put this _____ around me? I don't _____. _____ it's a game. Ha ha! He's telling me to put my _____ on the wall – yes, it's very _____. But where's that Amontillado? He said the cask was in _____, but I can't see it _____. And what's he _____ now?'

This is _____, and _____

because / does / front / great / minute / nearer / soon / work / worse

4 'Can't he see? It is happening in _____ of his eyes. Every day I feel _____ – I am getting _____ to death every _____. He looks at me all the time, but he _____ not see me. Now I know that his _____ love is not me – it is his _____. And _____ he loves his work more than me, I will _____ die . . .'

This is _____, and _____

boat / coffin / hands / remember / shaking / terrible / thank / wonderful

5 'What's happening? Why are you _____ me? Take your _____ off me! Am I – no, I'm alive! _____ God! They haven't buried me. Now I _____ – we came onto this _____ yesterday. This is a wooden bed, not a _____. Oh, _____ day! Perhaps now this _____ fear will leave me ...'

This is _____ who _____, and _____

47

2 **What did the young Englishman say to the Marchesa before the story begins? Put their conversation in the right order, and write in the speakers' names. The Englishman speaks first (number 4).**

1 _____ 'I will do anything in the world to show you how much I love you. Ask me anything – anything at all.'

2 _____ 'Yes. Then I will meet you at that last dark door.'

3 _____ 'I can never do that. If I leave him, my father will kill me.'

4 _____ 'Must you leave? Stay with me a little longer!'

5 _____ 'Ah yes, nothing can come between us then. But – how can I be sure of your love?'

6 _____ 'And then, when I have done what you ask, will you agree?'

7 _____ 'Then there is no hope for us. But if we cannot be together in life . . . there is another answer.'

8 _____ 'Very well, I will think of something. I will write to you – wait for my letter.'

9 _____ 'I love you more than life itself. And in death we will always be together.'

10 _____ 'No, I must go. You know that I want to be with you, but my husband . . .'

11 _____ 'Another answer? You mean . . . together in death? Do you really mean that? You love me so much?'

12 _____ 'Ah, your husband. Dearest, we cannot go on like this. Leave your husband! Come away with me!'

3 Use the clues to complete this crossword with words from the story (all the words go across). Then find two hidden words (four letters or more) in the crossword.

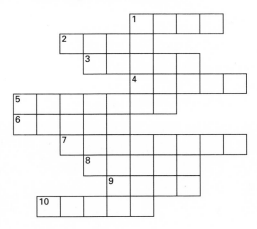

1 A little bit wet.
2 An alcoholic drink made from grapes.
3 A lot of metal rings joined together.
4 Water that comes from the eyes when you cry.
5 To take in air through your nose and mouth.
6 The part of a knife that cuts.
7 A party in the streets with music, singing, and dancing.
8 A place where a dead person is buried.
9 Like the shape of an egg.
10 The part of the body that pushes the blood around.

The hidden words are _____ and _____.

4 **Here is a new illustration for one of the stories. Find the best place to put it, and answer these questions.**

The picture goes on page _____, in the story _____.

1 Where has the young boy come from?
2 What news does he bring?
3 What has the narrator just realized?

Now write a caption for the illustration.

*Caption:*_____

5 Here are some new titles for the stories. Which titles go with which
   stories? Which titles do you prefer, and why? Now make up a title
   of your own for each story.

Love and Death in Venice   The Bed and the Blade
Montresor's Joke   A Picture of Life
Fire and Fear   The Last Wall
Painted to Death   Together in Death
The Only Answer   The Not-Dead
To the Edge of Death   Beautiful Dead Eyes
Everyone's Worst Fear   Carnival Terror
A Dream of Coffins

6 Which story did you find most frightening? Why? For you, which
   story was the most interesting, and which was the saddest? Why?

7 Look at the list below and imagine that you have to invite one of
   these characters to a party. Which one will you invite, and why?

The prisoner in Toledo   Montresor
The man who is afraid of burial alive   Fortunato
The young Englishman   The Marchesa
The Painter   The Painter's Wife

ABOUT THE AUTHOR

Edgar Allan Poe was born in 1809 in Boston, USA. His parents died when he was young, and he went to live with the Allan family in Richmond. He spent a year at university, and then two years in the army. In 1831 he moved to Baltimore, where he lived with his aunt and his cousin Virginia. For the next few years life was difficult; he wrote stories and sold them to magazines, but it brought him little money. But he did find happiness with Virginia, whom he married in 1836.

From 1838 to 1844 Poe lived in Philadelphia, where he wrote some of his most famous stories, such as *The Fall of the House of Usher* and *The Pit and the Pendulum*. Then he moved to New York City, where his poem *The Raven* soon made him famous. But Virginia died in 1847, and Poe began drinking heavily. He tried to kill himself in 1848, and died the following year.

Poe is often called the father of the modern detective story, because of his story *The Murders in the Rue Morgue* – the first story to show how the detective thinks. (The Mystery Writers of America give a prize called an 'Edgar' to the writer of the best mystery each year.) Poe wrote poetry, funny stories, and stories about time travel – a kind of early science fiction. But to most people the name Edgar Allan Poe means stories of death and madness, horror and ghosts. Most of the stories in this book have been filmed. There was a very early film of *The Pit and the Pendulum* in 1913, but the most famous film of this story was made in 1967, with the great horror actor Vincent Price.

ABOUT BOOKWORMS

OXFORD BOOKWORMS LIBRARY
*Classics • True Stories • Fantasy & Horror • Human Interest
Crime & Mystery • Thriller & Adventure*

The OXFORD BOOKWORMS LIBRARY offers a wide range of original and adapted stories, both classic and modern, which take learners from elementary to advanced level through six carefully graded language stages:

Stage 1 (400 headwords)	**Stage 4** (1400 headwords)
Stage 2 (700 headwords)	**Stage 5** (1800 headwords)
Stage 3 (1000 headwords)	**Stage 6** (2500 headwords)

More than fifty titles are also available on cassette, and there are many titles at Stages 1 to 4 which are specially recommended for younger learners. In addition to the introductions and activities in each Bookworm, resource material includes photocopiable test worksheets and Teacher's Handbooks, which contain advice on running a class library and using cassettes, and the answers for the activities in the books.

Several other series are linked to the OXFORD BOOKWORMS LIBRARY. They range from highly illustrated readers for young learners, to playscripts, non-fiction readers, and unsimplified texts for advanced learners.

Oxford Bookworms Starters	*Oxford Bookworms Factfiles*
Oxford Bookworms Playscripts	*Oxford Bookworms Collection*

Details of these series and a full list of all titles in the OXFORD BOOKWORMS LIBRARY can be found in the *Oxford English* catalogues. A selection of titles from the OXFORD BOOKWORMS LIBRARY can be found on the next pages.

The Canterville Ghost

OSCAR WILDE

Retold by John Escott

There has been a ghost in the house for three hundred years, and Lord Canterville's family have had enough of it. So Lord Canterville sells his grand old house to an American family. Mr Hiram B. Otis is happy to buy the house *and* the ghost – because of course Americans don't believe in ghosts.

The Canterville ghost has great plans to frighten the life out of the Otis family. But Americans don't frighten easily – especially not two noisy little boys – and the poor ghost has a few surprises waiting for him.

Dracula

BRAM STOKER

Retold by Diane Mowat

In the mountains of Transylvania there stands a castle. It is the home of Count Dracula – a dark, lonely place, and at night the wolves howl around the walls.

In the year 1875 Jonathan Harker comes from England to do business with the Count. But Jonathan does not feel comfortable at Castle Dracula. Strange things happen at night, and very soon, he begins to feel afraid. And he is right to be afraid, because Count Dracula is one of the Un-Dead – a vampire that drinks the blood of living people . . .

The Murders in the Rue Morgue

EDGAR ALLAN POE

Retold by Jennifer Bassett

The room was on the fourth floor, and the door was locked – with the key on the inside. The windows were closed and fastened – on the inside. The chimney was too narrow for a cat to get through. So how did the murderer escape? And whose were the two angry voices heard by the neighbours as they ran up the stairs? Nobody in Paris could find any answers to this mystery.

Except Auguste Dupin, who could see further and think more clearly than other people. The answers to the mystery were all there, but only a clever man could see them.

The Mystery of Allegra

PETER FOREMAN

Allegra is an unusual name. It means 'happy' in Italian, but the little girl in this story is sometimes very sad. She is only five years old, but she tells Adrian, her new friend, that she is going to die soon. How does she know?

And who is the other Allegra? The girl in a long white nightdress, who has golden hair and big blue eyes. The girl who comes only at night, and whose hands and face are cold, so cold . . .

Voodoo Island

MICHAEL DUCKWORTH

Mr James Conway wants to make money. He wants to build new houses and shops – and he wants to build them on an old graveyard, on the island of Haiti.

There is only one old man who still visits the graveyard; and Mr Conway is not afraid of one old man.

But the old man has friends – friends in the graveyard, friends who lie dead, under the ground. And when Mr Conway starts to build his houses, he makes the terrible mistake of disturbing the sleep of the dead . . .

Tales of Mystery and Imagination

EDGAR ALLAN POE

Retold by Margaret Naudi

The human mind is a dark, bottomless pit, and sometimes it works in strange and frightening ways. That sound in the night . . . is it a door banging in the wind, or a murdered man knocking inside his coffin? The face in the mirror . . . is it yours, or the face of someone standing behind you, who is never there when you turn round?

These famous short stories by Edgar Allan Poe, that master of horror, explore the dark world of the imagination, where the dead live and speak, where fear lies in every shadow of the mind . . .